BENEATH TREMENDOUS RAIN

Tony —

Best wishes for a
very Happy Birthday

with love from

Carol

MARTYN CRUCEFIX

Beneath
Tremendous Rain

ENITHARMON PRESS 1990

First published in 1990
by the Enitharmon Press
40 Rushes Road
Petersfield
Hampshire GU32 3BW

ISBN 1 870612 26 4

Set in 10pt Ehrhardt by Bryan Williamson, Darwen
and printed by
Antony Rowe Limited, Chippenham, Wiltshire

ACKNOWLEDGEMENTS

Some of these poems, or versions of them, have previously appeared in *Ambit, Between the Lines, The Gregory Poems Anthology* (Salamander Press, 1985), *Illuminations, The Literary Review, The London Review of Books, Outposts, Oxford Poetry, New Poetry from Oxford, Poetry Review, Poetry Wales, The Rialto* and *The Times Literary Supplement*. 'At the National Gallery' appeared in *Voices in the Gallery*, edited by Dannie and Joan Abse (Tate Gallery Publications, 1986). The first part of 'George and the Dragon' appeared in *Touchstones 1* (Hodder & Stoughton, 1987). 'Her Dream at Christmas' is included in *Contemporary Christian Poetry* (Collins, 1990). 'Rosetta' first appeared in a special edition of *Poetry Review* entitled *New British Poets*. 'South of Rosnakill' was a prizewinner in the Lancaster Literature Festival Competition, 1985. 'The Plait' was a prizewinner in the Kent Literature Festival Competition, 1988. 'Mikhael at Viksjön' was a runner-up in the 1989 WWF poetry competition and appears in *The Orange Dove of Fiji: Poems for the World Wide Fund for Nature* (Hutchinson, 1989). 'At Kavanagh's Bar, of course' was a prizewinner in the National Poetry Competition, 1989. Some of these poems were broadcast on BBC Radio Three, in May 1989, in a recording made at the South Bank Centre, London.

Contents

To sit in a great cold silence, and sing
out sweet with just our own warm breath:
that's some marvel, surely.

Blackcurrant Wine

'I have never heard any man mention his brother.'

The label's blotched with mould.
You wrote name and date four years ago
before you left for the other side of the world.
Now I lift the bottle out like an old document.
I'll read it with my tongue:
the glistening shot in the colander,
the sunlit kitchen, you absorbed in the task,
scales turning under a snowbank of sugar,
the steaming pulp, whiff of purifying acid,
the surgical look of siphoned fluids,
till like a row of old clocks the ruby jars
snore and murmur behind the sofa.

The cork sounds well as I pull it.
The smell is good –
but don't these old domestic labours
look absurd from where you are living now?
Like the clipped lawn, planted borders, vegetables
of the semi-detached we both grew up in?
Like me – come so many hundreds of miles,
through years of dizzying higher education,
shedding Dad's newspapers, diet, opinions,
to discover my first attempts in the garden
give me a shaved lawn, stocked borders,
in a sheltered corner four tomato plants.

Whereas you teeter on the edge of a jungle,
clinging to the skirts of a volcanic island
where it rains like you've never seen it before,
rain straight from the open hand of God,
no mediation from this world...

You record tapes to say you've settled well,
scrounged a hammock, veranda, table and chairs.
I hear the panting of your dog, the call
of strange birds as you circle the house
and talk of a quiet corner where the soil is good,
where you're trying a few tomato plants...

So to hell with the distance, the place and time.
I'll drink to you in bloody blackcurrant wine
till my temples itch and my stomach gapes
and each glass hits warmer and warmer there.
And when the bottle's gone, I'll be convinced
you talk with me, in blurred spirit at least,
lolling in a hammock beneath tremendous rain,
and laugh out loud when I try to suggest
that the fruit of our labour is ourselves.

Apples

My grandmother'd peel one, cut creamy slivers,
suck them from the knife, then show us pips
like cowering children stripped in their beds.

Or they'd be paraded into the warm room, lumpy
and cool from the pantry, shared equally round
from the greengrocer's stiff, brownpaper bags.

Or in shaking torchlight, plump in a foreign tree,
to be snatched unripe so the branches whiplashed
a heartstalling crash like the owner's backdoor

and we stumbled, laden, to a dark bolt-hole
in the hedge. They're still as coolly come-hither:
red-speckled, waxed, with that sweet cider reek,

though now I see the creased, dark navel below,
the bright flanks unevenly ruddy and blotched,
and where the shoulders hunch, I'm surprised

at the prickle of a woody, inedible stem.
Beneath this one, just a week longer in the bowl,
is some wrinkled twin, and my thumbs pressed

to its surface crimp the skin where a brown gash
on its shoulder has been healed with a scar.
It has softened and sweetened, remaining there.

Splinters

They'd always out in the end –
or so it was claimed – of their own accord.
Then why did he vividly recall
gouging at the wrinkled pad of his index
with a brutal pin picked from the sewing box?

Strange how the years go by
how less and less the need arises
to plough flesh after some buried speck.
Always black as a thorn whatever the source.
Driving a fork through dull clay,
he'd hook it finally with a braced pin

there

it would spring loose.
Confess itself. Cleansed,
he'd return both hands to the given task.

Water Music

*'I am not precise enough, what people
call precise. But words are not precise.
Divine fluidity, now that is truly precise.'*
                    Marc Chagall

1.
I am a potter whose habitation
is beside the water's music.
Its glittering's, its clear truckling's
endless fascination for me
might be the pull of like to like,
the rip-tides and rivers of my
almost nothing but water body.

Someone has said it's the lure
of oblivion, pressing me to bow
and snort the sharp stunning solid
of water into my head,
that with a brief flickering
of its long-fixed content
would scour my mind clean forever.

Perhaps. Or something still
unevolved, still amphibian, wanting
to be rid of this self-consciousness
that cripples me – to shiver
a moment with mother-of-pearl,
folding of currents, sands, slime,
the swordfight of refracted rays.

At least I know my fascination
for the fishmonger's wealth of silver,
that he is a diversion I often make,
though I cannot catch
any message his charges bring.

2.
Water has always been a god.
I fell in love with it as a boy,
would sit close by with the dusk,
determined to hook from it specimens
and secrets, calling to it
with words I'd let no adult hear.
Its glassy voices broke out
though too obscurely for a reply.

On the flaming beach at Thalassa,
where the crumbling glint of waves
marks the sea's edge, I once
wanted to meet it open-mouthed,
though not driven by any love
of the cold confines of the drowned.
I hoped that I might simply
receive the unbounded horizon.

At the graveyard there is a stone
set by a girl for her dead sailor:
Your ship, my love, is now mored
hed and starn for a fuldiew.
Below, the etched ship is lashed hard
to the quay – all else has grown
too old and faint to be understood.
The rain is rubbing her words away.

3.
Then it's everywhere with beauty,
at one with the darkness and moonlight
of the old poets for it transports us.
But I've seen it bending an iron bar.
The quiet cowl of October's fog confuses,
comes to question the formulations
we keep – like the traveller who told me:

16

the hills of Gomera disappear for days
till the rain washes its own window clear.
At Swirl Force, under whitening hammers
of waterfall, everything is broken loose
and then the clouds' anchors are weighed
and the dance starts up over the water:

every swollen-cheeked changeling face
stares at itself and floats away
with its glimpse on the heart of things.

4.
In my coercive dreams, there I am
pouring water into every available bowl
and setting them down as finished works.

I will have things as I want them,
though it is clear from whatever place
the water comes the bowls suffice –

though set to the river, their contents
fly to its night, are lost completely.
The river takes all that comes.

The river gives all that there is.
For I am a potter whose habitation
is beside the water's music, who is

driven to his creations just as
the river is to its own. When I clasp
the rounded belly of a brimming bowl

I carry something of water
that in my hands must leak away – see
its silver threads ceaselessly falling.

17

Potato Digger

As I struggle into my sleep-breaking voice,
he is building the house of my childhood
on earth he will soon make holy
by accident – with blood splashed from
a severed thumb because someone kicks
a clumsy breeze-block from an upper floor.

When the house is complete, the lawn laid
and curtains drawn, it's so easy to sleep.
But he's restless through all these years:
at tamping concrete, planing blonde curls
from a shelf, urging the push-mower on,
striding after its sprays of cut green.
My limbs tighten to a dream where he comes
to toss endless easy balls at the wicket.
Suddenly he stamps on the grass – the clash
of change in his pocket makes me scared
he's hurrying finally to catch me out...

But his hands still sort old pots of paint.
He levers uneven stones from the patio.
And it seems to me he has always stamped
the autumn garden with the seal of himself:
leaned forward, his careful right foot
pressuring the slanted fork to spill out
from dark earth a scatter of small potatoes,
chilled and white, exact and self-contained.

Searching for Thomas Helliker

*'He exchanged mortality for immortality
... The fatal catastrophe which led to
this unfortunate event is too awful to
describe.'*

(Inscription on Helliker's tomb, Trowbridge, Wiltshire)

Even tumbling out of Junior School
I felt, as if by instinct, as if history
could be imbibed from the local air,

that he was nearby. My suspicions
grew as we crocodiled down Church Street,
for the parish spire lorded it and he

was its secret. I suppose somebody
must have told me but thought the details
too dull to describe for such young ears,

though I was certain there were bones
close by and that was enough for one so
ignorant yet of the secrecies of things.

Only later did I discover the tomb,
neatly mixing its chiselled metaphor:
the thread of Helliker's life was cut

in the bloom of youth – which left me
with no image, though at least a location
in the great crumbling casket, set

under the churchyard's pines. Its text
was empty where I had hoped for answers;
keeping its secrets, it read only that he

was a hero who was killed for a crime.
So I built him in my mind to a martyr,
my county's Robin Hood. But such a flimsy

19

thing of fiction failed to cure the need
I had for truth. I turned to books
and found facts. *Tom Helliker was hanged*

at the age of nineteen, in 1803; he was
a shearman in Wiltshire's woollen mills;
took some part in anti-machinery mobs...

But when a man threatened the mill watchman
with a pistol, Tom was taken. Suspicion
was enough to kill and Helliker knew

who held the blame like a gun to his head
but never spoke; took his silence unbroken
up the scaffold's wooden stair. Surrounded

now with words, he is only his name,
for the flesh and the feeling – if that's
the true Tom Helliker – slips off through

silence and the best to be done is lay
name against name, to sustain a discontent
and resolve in this endless looking.

Mystery Dance

'I tried and I tried
and I'm still mystified.'
Elvis Costello

The icons were erected early:
rubbers, slags, garage, wank.
There was no sin
greater than ignorance.

*

I was one of those who knew nothing.
One of those who went into lessons
on Personal Relationships
and left in unshakeable disbelief.

Given a chance to post questions into a box
I wrote
      explain again how the man's seed
      gets inside the woman

and dropped it through the slot.

My vote for ignorance.
It fell onto a pile of identical others.

*

Even when the news broke in the abstract,
I couldn't attach it to the couples I saw
wrapped in each other on the bus.

So I came to believe
that I'd got stuck at a stage
– it was like missing a bus –

21

and one more was added to the growing list
of words I dared not use aloud
for fear they'd slap back in my face

(so those lessons had taught me something):

queer.

*

Riddiford would thump and tease
because he'd done it
and somehow knew I hadn't.

Was it a change in the face?
A different kind of walk?
Each small bush of hair in the shower?

*

I held her gloved hand in the dark
and wheeled my bike back to her house.

I'd stop and kiss her on the mouth
five streetlamps from *The Black Horse.*

The Black Horse galloped by.
Her hand was wrapped deadwood in mine.

My head wouldn't turn. My mouth wouldn't talk.

*

We stopped in the darkened porch.
Immediately dogs began to howl.
Someone inside thoughtfully blinded us
with the porchlight.

In desperation, I kissed her cheek goodnight.
It felt like a perfumed cloth.
It would feel nothing.

I pedalled away,
nailing the best face I could on the evening:
pleased that I'd not stooped
as some might have done to a clumsy grapple.
I respected her; she'd respect that.

She told me later she tore upstairs and wept.

*

The first time came sooner than later:
clumsy, painful, cold, unprotected.

I remember a dressing-table,
a mirror, a blue plastic brush.
The bed creaked in the far angle of the wall.

Hot and sore all night long,
I had to leave early – a holiday job –
and floated to work quite simply
on the strength of that struggling
bungled affair.

Sugar in Banana Sandwiches

'Still something of the child in you'
she says. I find that hard to swallow
and blithely offer this half-deceit.
It's less the sweetness of the thing
I like, it's more the melting crunch
it makes of every mouthful, hidden
in the pliable cool mass of flesh.

And I thought I was out on my own.

The unfamiliar boy who cycles past,
his chain clanking against the guard,
dissolves in rain and we three children
lie warm in our beds, folded securely –
gutters threatening with blown rain,
while a rusty sign rhythmically creaks
its years-old *safe now safe now* sound.

Sometimes nothing of my own seems new.
I push a steering wheel with a careful
right hand like holding a pen – like Dad.
Where my brother sleeps, his body's angles
are the measure of mine. When I let go
with a nervous laugh, I hear the voice
of my mother's father clearing plates...

So little's lost. Even in the heat of love
when I'm most myself, I wonder what it is
I echo here in the flex of this muscle?
The press of my hand? Or who, before me,
has known the way my back has bent?
Or drawn these mouthfuls of air I breathe
to fill out these thirty years of flesh?

Midsummer at High Laver

*(The philosopher, John Locke, is buried at
All Saints' Church, High Laver, Essex.)*

1.
I've beaten roads dusty with summer to be here.
Left the two of them, hands held then waving
before the groomed hedge. Both looked older
again, walking Wiltshire fields where slopes
have browned and stained poppy-red in places
like a bloody graze across sun-burned knees:
a hurt from those days quickly soothed by Mum;
bragged up later to a great exploit for Dad.
The two of them...
                    Absent-minded,
my body alone has felt the pedals, held the wheel
as I've unearthed older and younger days
as precisely as those thumb-nail steps carved
in the solid encyclopaedia I homeworked from,
perched at a desk on the edge of my bed.

2.
I bolted knowledge then.
The cuckoo, beak biggest part of itself.
A schoolboy stealing coinage from lucid books,
laying instalments on a life of smart logic.

Now I drive through the fecundity of earth,
through these hectares of flowering potato,
white constellations adrift on undulating green,
with the conviction that this is a watershed:

so much of the talk at home is of death;
how do I brazen that out with an argument?

3.

I've come to where jet-sprays of irrigation
relieve the cracked fields of hot midsummer.
I've come in self-conscious homage to High Laver,
burial place of that logical father
whose stodgy book of rational commonsense
sprung the tradition I've clung to long enough.

A laburnum sapling creaks in its rubber thong
at a stake where I stalk the graveyard to find
the oldest stone...Always I've done this,
yet surreptitiously, plotting false explanations
for myself as it's the heart that says
this is a powerful place, where generations
of local good and ill in swathes
have gone down like centuries of grass.

4.

But I forget what I'm here for.
Stood beside this body volume of displaced earth
piled weeks ago beneath the trees –
on that last day some stranger's beloved mother
had more flowers than she ever dreamed of.

The blown wreaths outstare me.
In a blink aside there's more than I feared
of the two of them, wrapped against coming cold:
Dad, hands stuffed in his pockets,
standing off on his own; Mum, struggling
to peg out snapping shirtfuls of wind.

5.
I watch the flailing mare's-tail, the jet-stream
spray of the irrigator beside the church.
Its white angle above the potato fields
seems to crumple to a vaporous nothing, yet
a judder slams sudden clouds of fizzing spray.
It's drenching some different sector of the field,
this drained, tearful, flowering place.

Drunk

Heart still patters with last night's poison.
The spiteful world squats on each optic nerve,
wrenches my head towards the blaring window.

As if my brain had snapped its stalk –
it steadies queasily
as oily water slopped clumsily round a tank.

A mallet-blow belled over my left eye all morning.
Worse – it faded hour by hour,
a barbed stiletto skewered from the skull.

I've hung for hours
over the hurtful purity of the lavatory,
its white, deepening, accusatory lens.

My mind possesses all the sharpness
of a fluffy, liquefying peach in a dish.
I feed it deliberately with scenes

of long tawny glasses slid across the table-spills.
Hands receive them of their own accord.
But at the touch of liquid to lip, a trap-door

bangs open, brain's a torrent of sand
rocketing from my mouth
to make the only eye that sees me blind.

The House on the Hill

1.
Night and morning, we check for scorpions
no bigger than spiders. When discovered
they must be firmly stamped on.

But none of this can spoil my sense
of indulgence because I'm raiding memory
furiously for secrets to share with you.

Men don't talk like this as a rule.
Is it the foreign country? The cheap wine?
The slack hours of uninterrupted sun?

Or that we've been spring-loaded so long
we snapped together in this dull company?
As with scorpions, we're on tenterhooks.

2.
I'm the late-comer here, the one-too-many,
asleep on the bellying sofa with the tap-drip,
crickets, the cracks of the shrinking house,

nightly checking each day's revelation:
my love of the uncertain man in you.
Nothing's said. *Did you sleep well?*

3.
We sneak to town while the others quarrel.
Where blurting mopeds occupy the streets,
we get closer on beer and talk, talk, talk.

At dusk, we swerve and clank our way back
to the house on rusting, childish bikes.
Each breath is laughed and we're both in love

with being drunk and happy and propelled
down this warm night. Shadowy vineyards
spread themselves beneath a faultless moon.

4.
But we're back inside too soon. Both suddenly
aware we've pedalled unconsciously hard,
panting, flushed, legs trembling with the hill.

At the meal-table later, I touch your thigh
to stop you from bickering with them...
This is our affair. I'll have no-one hurt you.

In Memory of Jeremy Round

1.
You lived a strange short life.
Breezed so quickly through mine
it's only now I see how deep
you touched, a taste of something

tartly clean. You moved on, grew
famous for daring to smoke
monkfish fillets in a wok
over a fortune-telling of tea.

Cheered by admiring colleagues
for the clarity with which you
explained how to separate a mango
from its skin and stone.

All the culinary prizes tumbled
to you as quickly as the doors
of London opened – as quickly
as the weight went on...

Whoever saw you suffer long
the English disease? Endlessly
unbuttoned I remember you,
though we never dined al fresco

near Antioch, nor tossed back
West Coast rock oysters, hurried
them down with a glass of bubbles.
All my puritanical doubts –

shocked at the world in whose sky
you were the fastest rising star –
they were blown so cleanly away
by your sheer celebratory hunger.

Everybody remembers you smiling.
Serious in the obituary snap
from six years back, I'd forgotten
what a sexy mouth you had.

You were that rare thing, a good man –
though not to the bishop's liking.
You said: happiness will be caviar
and unpasteurised brie in heaven.

2.
Nights on George Street, when words clouded
and breathed-air froze hard in our nostrils,
we met in Oxford with the other hopeful scribes,
behind leaded windows in the Old Fire Station.
All that bitter winter you buttoned and belted
a heavy gaberdine so tightly round your middle,
spreading already...Even trussed up, your
cultured Falstaff-spirit couldn't be dampened.
You were good for us – heady and deadly serious
as we were, you persuaded that poetry's sister
arts were food and sex. We all studied hard.

I remember you praised my poems but always
had your doubts. We'd wrangle inconclusively
between the beers and crossfire from Tom,
elder statesman who'd slip quiet, glittering
poems from his tackle bag like fish; from Helen,
whose pages always seemed typed under earthquake
conditions, whose baggy poems had more passion
than most of us could muster; from Peter's
exactitude, schooled on a diet of science, he held
each piece like a prism till it shed eloquent
rainbows; from Bill and Keith, the ferocious
tyros, the university wits, who minced nothing
but their language into strange sweet things;

from Paul, whose poems were amazed not to find
themselves loosed into a more graceful age than
the one we live in. God! We were going to take
the poetry world by storm! We'd put it to rights,
marching on a diet of your invention. Jeremy, you
earned the right to imagine us, desk-bound now,
back in the old ways, chewing on unproductive pens
dark-browed and anxious for a fitting elegy.

3.
In spring
I called at your house in Osney,
the place where Chaucer's Alison
cried her sexy 'Tee-hee!'
and had her arse kissed.

You were preparing a chicken
and as you talked
a surgeon's hand wielded a razor-knife
and flew so quickly
over the creamy, pimpled skin
that it offered itself up, seemed to open
perfect nicks, exactly placed
for the garlic cloves
you pushed gently into each
and patted shut with a slap.

Finished, we talked again:
how you enjoyed my poems
yet you wanted them always
to gird themselves more,
to snatch up a swig of the wicked
and bellow YES.

4.
Why must the good go under the ground?
I mean those who are as full of life
as my friend, portly Jeremy Round.
He wielded a pen as sharp as his knife.
He loved the world, craved its taste –
so he put it on around the waist.

Salmon, wine and the rankest cheese,
limpid Mozart, Berg and Bach:
he killed himself trying to squeeze
everything in. He made himself a rack
of pleasure, eager to blow the spark
of life before it all went dark.

I sit here and still catch my breath
because I remember him so well.
His every action said: screw death!
Get the best you can or go to hell!
Days should be funny, sexy, intense –
sheer delight makes perfect sense.

He'll never, I know, accept the part,
but I'm sure he'd relish the cheek
if I write him with an honest heart.
Listen! let me make this master speak:
Laughter, love, the senses are profound.
Drink deep, remember, Jeremy Round.

Marrow

It's armoured, a stellar shape, each stiff
outstretched arm crowded with spicules.
Lifts thick maple-leaves that are rough-
sticky as a dogfish skin with invisible barbs.
Milk-white rose thorns stand a stiff guard
beneath the ribbed gantry of each vein.

And the beauty behind the fortifications?
From the heart, tiny green candles come
bearing mute, in-turned, lemon flames.
Their gathering tumescence for a few hours
breaks open to a glossy, silken yellow,
splays extravagant pleasure-pavilions
for the sun. Hairy pollen carriers delve
in each throat where the stigma-curd swells
on a rod thrust back through lemon lips.
There, furred, green-striped fruit will begin.

It's quickly finished. Flower ribs suddenly
hold only bruised, discolouring fabric,
flaccid as a rotten sail. Each bloom knots
into itself and droops its retiring head.
But the young marrows continue to swell.
Leave them long enough and they'll reach
forty pounds – but cut them early and sweet.
Stuff with tomatoes, celery, garlic cloves,
bake smothered in cheese. A bottle of wine.
Make a celebration. Make love. Sleep well.

A Cat

On the step, cat is a banshee screaming
to come in. The irresistible argument
of his fur and needle-bones is a chain
around my ankles. He breaks the iron bar
of my will like a straw because cat is
a strongman who rakes across the hallway
with strides of elephantine deliberation,
invades the kitchen with such a presence
the everyday shrinks back to clear a space
as a crowd's waves ripple away from where
the assassin struck. A second curling
yell for milk which he stoops to batter
into submission with a pinkish flickering.
Then he rips open the sofa for a game.

Immediately wants to be out again,
under the step, where he has laid out
the delicacy of a mouse...

Cat genuflects before it, bows, lifting,
begins a quiet massage of its damp head
with his mouth. His sides pant a little
with the effort of love. Softened, preoccupied
eyes lift to my call and show the mouse
is headless and his own bloodied whiskers
like a clumsy cosmetic on a child's face.
The calm stare lowers, head now dipping
in a gentle affirmative to the crisp ticking
of bones as if a timepiece had yielded
to the sure touch of the craftsman.
Then the quiet kissing of bursting sacs.
Cat's complete gaze strokes the garden.
Unseen, the blood's red stain below the step.

Barkbröd

'The power of the word CANCER is overwhelming.
It drives out the light and darkness, pervades
every waking moment... You can no longer
think rational thoughts or act with common sense.'

1.
It is the rawness
of my own throat
that forebodes.

So little else has
been altered, yet
everything's realigned

as if from without.
My peasant-thoughts
mix bitter bark

with dull flour
to eke life out.
They recognise

the violent-sudden
clarification
of their strength,

its cropped boundary.
Breath shortens.
Sweet Betjeman,

black-eyed Larkin:
these two dead men
alive on a screen

to discuss poetry,
the intimacies
of panic and pain.

And a malignancy
in the songbird's
weak throat severs

the transference
from hand to hand.
The grandparents

of my young bride
pass along these
pallid, frost-blue

roses on bone china.
Whether shelved or
to hand, they chill me:

their stark reaction
to our modish
wisdom, our shallow

unquestionable
optimism...
Take up the bitterness

of this bread
brush every crumb
towards the sink

and douse your plate.
Baptise and scour
each blue-ice rose.

2.
The first peculiarities of this year's
snowlight break up the bedroom glass.

There's a crackle of news in the kitchen.
All is well. Yet the difficulty is this:

to convey information which is true,
while avoiding fear which is unnecessary,

yet maintain hope which is essential.
In a mess of sensual pleasure and death

it rose obediently to hand as I soaped
my breasts, in my left, quite low down.

Unmistakable. How long have I nursed
this featureless clod over my heart?

Water gems and drains from my feet.
The radio chuckles at my trembling.

3.
What remains to be done
but retire into some
Ainola of the mind,
glimpsed down a track

of snow, pine, a refuge
still as a blown flute.
I wake at night thirsty
and from the window,

across tangled gardens,
a yellow light burns,
sketching the grid
of dull-bricked walls.

But I sink to sleep
still unresolved
whether this midnight's
oil is some illness,

vocation, compassion,
or the absent-mindedness
we fearfully deny.
Your thinned hair now

combed neatly back
behind fleshy ears.
And how is the throat?
Nervy artist's hands

flutter about the chin.
Those pale eyes of yours
gaze hard at my room,
at this ceiling's rose

across my shoulders.
I guess you're slow to be
moved, yet once begun
a relentless nature

like time or weather.
It's a gaze to outlast
any physique: this slip
of a thing, your strength.

4.
*This clod in my breast
wears a tight
black neckerchief.*

It must be evil
that I think of it
as a child...

Dark nights running
I dream of him
rapping gently

against the door
— our bedroom door —
till I answer.

So she speaks
as we journey south
out of London,

through the suburbs'
assembled brambled
tussocky plots,

bright washing
collecting the sun
as it drops

long shadows
to meet us both
on the allotments.

Vitality sickens me
with fierce envy
and the *why? why?*

Across the carriage
a brash student
absently rearranges

his big thighs.
Two powerful hands
murder the fruit

he cleanly eats.
*I let him in
over the threshold.*

These backs of houses
so ordinary
that reassurance

ought to flow
from them. Yet
we both move here

as an illustration,
a shadow,
quite regardless:

of how a charming boy
will come to the door
from without,

how you bend to him
just as he's hulking
through transformation

into a killer
in our bedroom
who bolts you upright,

over and over,
screaming unrestrained
beside me.

House with Ghost

At night there is a woman
who cries here.
She wakes me to complete darkness.
When the television is extinguished
I become aware of her sobbing
teasing the boundary of hearing.

My ghost never laughs;
is never mischievous.
Her sadness descends on me.
It is beyond all reasoning
that these so few, so small
rooms should house
such strength for sorrow.

A Woman of Kokoschka's

My obsessions flower brash as amaryllis
every once in a while. They root in one night's
tangled dreaming round a woman, a man.

But this quiet tristia's been fashioned
solely for her from scraps of hours spent
picking through bookshelves to no purpose.

She is unaware of my desire for her dozen
chalked lines on the page, of my gratitude
that this unflinching gaze can't taint her,

tempt her to betray herself with a show.
She has the flesh of a sensual woman –
but it's not her. She refuses outright:

left arm raised, the armpit's black with hair.
Unshapely creasemarks map a belly that's
rucked by the one raised knee as she sits

so her slit-navel is lifted to the light.
She's unmetaphorical woman, immune,
whose dropped head gazes on her thighs.

Her body drifts on some slow Amazon within,
secure from admirers, from the artist, from me,
from the crawl of years. See, how she sits,

undressed too simply to be anything less
than the residue we dare to hope is left
when we are rubbed away. I see the proof

in her ribby trunk, the small visible breast,
the buttock squeezed by her own firm weight
where it's caught pressed to an imaginary floor.

Rehearsal for a Requiem

Each night she floats back at ten, head bobbing
on some glistening current of song
burst from the dam-break of a hundred urgent throats.

But this evening – though the fumbled lock's shot
back and chill air blasts in, the same hum
of the same well-oiled voice – it's different.

Her footsteps hurry beyond my door
towards the bathroom and before the ritual soprano
fills the flattering acoustic of enamel tile,

the seat is dropped, a zipper flies
and an almighty fart ripples the air:
such a thundering of the indefatigable past

it blue-bludgeons our few rooms. Only then
from the dying fall, lifts a quavering voice
with the sound of stars on such a frosty night:

Out of the deep. Out of the deep have I called.

Drowned Shelley

'Nothing of him that doth fade,
But doth suffer a sea-change
Into something rich and strange.'
(Inscription on Shelley's Memorial, Rome)

Just a frail craft and the obstreperous sea
and sky conspiring. No justice of poetry
or martyrdom. Just storm, the thunder's sound,
a sheeting rain and the swell rearing around
you suddenly. Then, it would not have taken
long till between lips and tongue once shaken
only by the to and fro of breath, salt water
ran steadily in a flow that did not falter
till you had drunk enough. Floating facedown
as if intent on the sea's remoter world, found
more true finally than this of air, with no eyes
you mock Milton at last with a gaze that lies
where you thought it should: in the human mind.
Its images are before you: the dappled, wave-lined
sea-bed shifts its green and gold marble there,
displaying its wasted beauty. And in your hair,
soaked in brine and tangled on your head,
where it's dried by the Italian sun, as if shed
show the salt's sharp crystals, found
like facts unaccompanied by the mind's sound.
Where the subtle imagination once held sway,
in the brain's cup, small things push their way
from place to place and perhaps discover
drowned thoughts or with their work uncover
fragments of a poem. But now, completely
at one with the waves, you cannot tell me
how it is, cradled with such concern and care,
they bear you shorewards and once there
nudge you as if in encouragement to wake
and gently walk on the sand. The waves take
their leave and leave the unrecognisable dead
to dry, Keats' Odes waiting to be read
in a pocket where you pushed them. Far above,

46

gulls wheel where Mary comes freighted with love,
objectless and unrequited now, where Trelawney
and Byron come and beside the brilliant sea,
burn you: bellying smoke marks a sea-change
already assumed, from something rich and strange.

South of Rosnakill

Stopping at Broad Water as the sun fell,
we saw what later seemed to have been
a sentry – an outriding white swan –
a solitary, paddling the setting stream
of golden light and catching its fire.

Following the road at the shore's edge,
the sun's bright blaze even threw
a gilding across the angles and planes
of a grey factory – the scenery's flaw –
with its labouring trucks, sacks and bins.

Then we saw swans had gathered there
in great numbers, clustered like stones
in the golden flood; drifting smoothly
across the shallows; standing in a sheen
of mud; like still, low fires on the sand.

So much assembled beauty and so serene
ought to open paths to the places of myth
and dreams – I stared only, open-eyed
as a camera to take it down, though deeper
the dark patterning into words began.

And works still, though driving on we saw
the grimy factory was a bakery whose
leavings, fed out to the water, had drawn
the birds. No more mysterious calling.
Their shapely fires gild and jewel still.

Her Dream at Christmas

She went back to church after years –
not penitent, rather curious
about how things had altered there –
but she wasn't prepared for this.

In place of the old style communion,
where thin priests would grimly spare
a dry biscuit, and a sniff of wine
was all the drink they'd ever share

...instead of that, she saw this:
there was nut-loaf on the choir-stall,
with each prayer book a banana split.
There was quiche, crab salad, lemon fool.

There on the font sat a turkey roast,
parsnips, carrots, sprouts spilled over.
The whole church was a perfect feast!
On the pews stood raspberry pavlova.

And where the faithful knelt in line
drinks were unsteadily dispensed
from a box of chilled Italian wine.
She knew the price must be immense.

She fled back home and found a place
of hunger – rooms of emptiness.
Then she fell asleep for forty days
and woke with this need to confess.

View of Sancta Sophia

Head unorthodoxly draped in filthy net,
I lean from our hotel window.
The morning sweeper spirits his pile
of rotten fruit, string, plain dirt and paper
under parked cars as if they're magic carpets.
I ask aloud if you'd call that faith.
There's no reply. You're sleeping again.
A few hours abroad and we're already reeling.

This first room is a hundred shades of brown.
The midday oven will stretch us naked
across the bed feeling helplessly randy.
But it's too hot even in imagination.
We'll listen to the cross-legged melon-seller
libating his pitch with tap-water.

The symbols are easy enough here
where Christ is a second-rate prophet.
Above the rooftops' higgledy sunlights,
god's thin fingers indicate the sky.
Each has a swollen joint which will unleash
a quivering swoop of sound...
They wake us at inconvenient hours.
But the heat is passing. Soon we'll be able
to start work on each other's pleasure.

Later, I might open the tap
(much later, when the light has gone)
A cool swathe drawn from Istanbul's buried cisterns
into the cracked white ghost of the sink.

On the Silk Road

The poor man beside me
wears his heavy spectacles
as I would a stethoscope:
a faint air of embarrassment,

a great deal of care.
He believes the government
is good, but it will unearth
his people to ensure

the foreigners a free reign.
Within years, it will happen.
But tell this to the woman
astride a nerveless donkey

(she might be his wife)
wrapped like a parcel
to the sliver of her eye.
She hobbles out of the Old Testament

into the village
like a prompt illustration.
These people are resilient,
says Franz. *So proud.*

All that's irrefutable
is the swift Mercedes coach,
its horns blurting
at each rickety cartload

of thistles as it tackles
the margin of tarmac and dust.
At nightfall local artists
scrabble at their guitars.

It's then the animals
take the stars for themselves.
When drunks in white slacks
tailored to the Occident

are stumbling arm in arm
about the dance floor
and we, my sweetheart,
amongst our implications,

are breathless also
since we are compelled
to relive the past day's
roll-call of achievements,

our petty blustering
at the terminus,
our *don't ever shout at me
in public again!*

No Messages

With these bursts of dawn blindness
there's a greasy shock-head of hair
at the white mirror each morning.
A speck of marmalade is caught
beside the lips in three days' growth.
A shrew nose, sunken cheeks and eyes,
and there, the left cheek blemished.
Each uncertain donation of cash
or spirit becomes more difficult,
less frequent, till I see I'm stowed
away at last where we may all
be destined to be dead men's bones.

I'm set down in the rivet-punched
gun-grey corridors below and hear
the roars of the tiger, our cargo.
The bright world of water vibrates
all around as the sailors above go
about their automatic businesses.
No messages. I send none. Below deck
we nurse a black and brackish death.
It's not rats – yet something's tugged
my conscience as if to say *it's you
who will murder.* We meet only at
each brief port and ought to settle.

Yet like the tiger's gravelling roar,
thundersigns bound blackly towards us
from the islands. These rags of sail,
flickering ribbons in the sudden gale
(what in the world does this mean?),
black trunks of water-spouts thump
like mines, spin, bend, buckling pillars.
Surf is a chaos of stars, sulphur-
flakes across our lights as if launched

upon the tiger's bellowing breath.
The quick brine crawls inch on inch
through fur, limbs, throat and eyes.

Then blue sharks hang in the blue ocean
once more. A loose rag's been flung
over a side-rail where I try to purge
my body of its malcontents.
Horizons tip and slither around me.
I lean back. The milky new paring
of the moon talks sense: put all this
to good use, to waste and want not
and resolve now to thump this tub
of a table since everything I touch
(what in the world does this mean?)
instantly fumbles into fragments.

Watching Tennis in the Summer of 1986

Players blow on their hands and prepare to receive.
Since April I spend days mapping family history
though fraying palm-lines suggest I'll never marry

or have children. The Registry's monumental books
mark out the logic of birth, match and death's
simple ruling across remote tennis summers.

It's frightening. This picked-bone childlessness,
infidelities sans issue as if I already lived a war
economy of love to the quibbling accompaniment

of neighbours angry that so many can make so
little difference. What has happened to us all?
I am worn out today under the old compulsion

where there's no end to imagining all I love
a hissing clinker lobbed through cracking space.
The champion drops her bright face into a towel.

You see this formica table? A bad joke of blood-red
hearts with umbrellas. No strawberries, no cream.
Now the childless are glued to the flight of a ball.

The Nurseryman in his Garden

1. *The Nurseryman*

See how my wife hasn't bothered to open
the curtains. It's three o'clock. She must be bad.
She thinks I don't know what it costs her
to steal a glance at me outside, to brave
these fifty feet of open space, her weak legs
trembling with the sick terror in her belly,
knotting ever closer round her heart...
I'll cut some chrysanthemums to please her.
My flowers always please her.

Years ago she'd tell me how it felt.
She'd say a bulb will sometimes come up blind
no matter how carefully you've set it down.
It's the way of plants. There's no cure at all.
But it's not only her. Still as poor as Adam,
there's just one thing I have that's in demand
and it's not right that a man who's spent life
tending the soil into flower should gain nothing
but a touch for dressing death in glad rags
with some careful blooms on a wire frame...
I've found a natural talent for wreathes.
My one extravagance: that I can charge
higher prices than most and though Christmas
is a boon (when my great medals hang on
so many bolted doors), yet it's the year-round trade
in bereavement that keeps this place afloat.

I'd plans once. A shop, new greenhouses, a son.
Now I'm forced to take on a series of young lads
who help me out. They're all more or less sullen.
This one's so quiet, although he chats to girls
across the hedge, as they all have done –
all playing the working-man, hands dirtied,
with the jangle of my money in their pockets.
This one trails his radio around all day long

as if he can't stand the sound of himself.
Doesn't work hard. See where he goes now,
slipping down beside the sheds. No radio today.
Well, he's happy enough on one-fifty an hour...

I must cut some chrysanthemums to please her.
Tomorrow we start to grub out the thorn hedge.

2. *The Boy*

That quid-fifty an hour's
an insult if he wanted a good job
out of me – who suffocated under glasshouses
where the air's thick as a wet soup
you drink, not breathe, like a broth
of pollen, peat, cells dividing like fury –
where one step through the outer door
is like diving into an ice-box –
the relative cool of what's really
the sweating heat of mid-July –
where he'd make me spray a thousand chrysanths,
pumping the bottle to pressure –
lugging it, heavy as a crippled leg,
up and down his untidy rows.

We hardly ever spoke –
just 'how many hours?' and 'how's your father?'
and endlessly
'good lad', 'good lad' so much
it makes me wonder what he really thinks –
of her, maybe – who's frightened of open spaces –
who I've never seen
though sometimes a curtain will stir
like the bottom of a pond with her –
I don't know
if he cares or not –

though when we tore up the thorn hedge
a month or so ago, I looked up
and caught him staring at the front window –
curtains drawn at two in the afternoon –
and I swear she wasn't there.

Then, for once, relieved
when the girls came by – though I never know
what to say to them –
                              'Hello'
'Where's the old man, gardener?'
'You live near here?'
                              'Yes' –
then back to the hothouses
where huge pipes twist and discolour with heat –
or better still
down past the sheds – away out of sight –
lie back against the folds of corrugated iron
and wank myself off –
legs cocked in the air like a grasshopper,
screaming at the girls in clammed silence –
till once – a blink of the hall curtain –
her face – a white kite, transfixed –
severed as the curtain fell to
heavy as a door.
I will never go back.

3. *The Wife*

I sit beside a beautiful maidenhair fern.
It likes my darkness, is dank, spreads slowly.
I count my books, silent on their long shelves.

I'm dying of a pure old age, not experience.
I was not always so understanding – accusations
and resentment shouted him into the garden.

58

We have not given each other all we'd hoped.
I name children, true pleasure, company...
I've felt such horror at what lies beyond

the window, where even clothes on the line,
blown by an uncontrollable wind, cardigans
undone and swept open, my slacks kicked wide

are too much to bear. He has devoted himself
too much to the fertility of row upon row
of plants and had less and less for me.

But we're long past the allotment of blame.
For years, he'd bring chrysanthemums
to me and watch like a child while I shook

earwigs in the sink, flushed them out of sight.
An absurd ritual which I long for, absurdly,
since it ended these past four or five years

before the hedge was removed to make up beds
of carnation. And we've no boys here now –
as if a supply-line had suddenly gone dry.

Don't parents have children nowadays?
They all blur into one – that particular one
who left quickly. Why do I think of him?

He's forgotten me. Or does he have a wife?
And a child? I remember descending the stairs,
past the grave-quiet telephone, with a jug

of water in my hand. I thought I heard
one of the cats, opened a sliver of curtain.
I would do this all over again...

See the boy slumped against the shed
legs crooked and splayed, one hand flickering
on his belly as if dealing a deck of cards –

but with such unrestrained violence.
He saw me. Gave the look of one who has been
interrupted – annoyance, much more than

the guilt I'd expect. I dropped the curtain,
then wanted to open it again – and it's that
which fills me now when I think of 'life'

and then I see myself – the dry, pressed flower
I once found in a borrowed library book,
squeezed out now, frightened of the light.

Elegiac for Fiona Glass

What was it that killed you? Just a trace
of gas and then (I was wrongly told) fire,
consuming, blowing flesh from bone, your face
snapped featureless, everything laid bare.

On that night I knelt in an emptying bath –
the warmth of the water swirling away
on all sides, draining off into death,
cooler and cooler – too frightened to say

to myself: this is how it would have been,
last seconds of consciousness gone in fog
and pain...I wanted to see it gentle, clean.
All I heard was the water's appalling gag.

And now tonight they are flying you back.
I've since learned you died in no fire-blast
but in sleep and gas. The earth is still dark
now it has you, unharmed, stone-cold at last.

Would you have understood? I know elegy
is meant to rise gently onto firmer ground
and shed its grief, but I give no apology
for failing, though your poem may not stand.

Mikhael at Viksjön

They stopped bombing the lake with lime
a year ago. The helicopters stopped coming.
You see where it's unnaturally dark;
daylight vanishes undiminished to the bed.
I think of it as an absence of energy –
accepting everything and like the old
giving nothing back.

I hate them for it. The grey men who say
it's the British unfurling filthy flags,
blurting a language so strong it burns trees,
blackens the water, scalds memory clean
for a better world. Well, I've seen it:
I dreamed a sun above a dry, scuffed land
bleached white but for two mud-dark shelters,
lean-tos like wedges laid flat to the ground.
That was all. I tore every useless permit
I had, threw the scraps to the lake
wanting to see them shrivel into flame
as they touched the water.

I used to swim from the speckled rocks.
Swallows flashed above like fish through a lake.
First signs came with bright weather.
The water a lacklustre eye squeezed
under a skyline of pine like quills.
At the beach, the white bellies of perfect bream.

Then the helicopters waited till dusk
to drop their white loads crashing
and fizzing on the lake,
scrawling its surface like a mist.
Now they've stopped bombing and I no longer
think I see the tell-tale rings of rising fish.
Their splash would always hush the lake.
Now there is only a more difficult quiet,
one I use only for the anger which will not
follow the daylight to the bottom
but which comes clattering back at me off
the blackened water, louder and clearer,
louder and clearer!

Painting a Gale

The familiar need to rule and trim
keeps me indoors. I sit by the window,
dabbling gouache with nervy strokes.
At my elbow, a loose sash rattles
and fans a draught across the room:
a whiff of rain and new-crushed wood.
Dustbins lose their clattering heads.
Old Hughes' fence suddenly buckles –
hammer in hand, he's instantly there
repairing the dam, his backyard boiling
over the doorstep with imagined water.

Above the street's ruin of umbrellas,
a dark shape is stealthily adrift
across the churning, luminous sky –
a plane of wood, man-high, shoulder-wide,
being flung by the wind like balsa.
A gust flicks it clear of the roof.
It drops plumb as an unopened door
and thunders inches into the pavement
at the toes of a startled couple –
upright, quivering, an unexpected choice.
They're appalled on its threshold.

El Caudillo

I relished the moment that had waited
almost fifty years and pissed on the memory
of Las Raices. Slowly, I'd driven
the same road the black Mercedes took,
the climb towards the interior
and the island's sleeping volcano.
At Las Raices the ground slopes still
under thickening layers of needles
beneath the strictly vertical pines
that lift to attention like an army.

1936. As the car slid to a halt,
a voice from behind me took the trees
to illustrate a nation of proud men
and murmured on, uninterrupted,
through the click and cough of the doors.
They strode away, leaving me the creak
of the engine cooling as they walked
to and fro under the flickering pines –
el caudillo followed like a cat
with his mob of clamouring starlings.

I'm glad I found their garish monument
in the wrong place, too far up the hill.
It displays *pax* beside battle-shields
and spears in a red like a blaring horn.
I emptied myself behind it. Not in front.
Even now, when the paint is peeling,
the war forgotten, years since the life
seeped out of his body bit by bit
as we watched in those last long months
– I'm not sure it would be safe.

And is that the sum of my learning?
It was always clear nobody believed
we drivers ever talked about such things.
But I remember the *bosque de la Esperanza*,

a radiator burst, a car was sent for him.
I talked with Alisio as we were towed back,
how there were times – and that was one –
for a clearing away, a clean sheet,
setting out on a new road, convinced
of making a clear break with history.

That man Alisio... did he ever return
enough changed by what happened
not to dare piss openly on this place?
Was he here with them on that day?
Perhaps he never saw them come striding
back to the cars, heads down, kicking
up flares of pine needles before them
so you knew they'd decided to do it,
like dumping an old car, as I imagined,
cleanly in some quiet place.

But as I wound the Mercedes back to town,
not a word was spoken behind me.
I was frightened, too fast to the corners.
I'd expected talk, argument, plans...
Though it's fifty years late, now I see
they couldn't expel the sharp scent
of pine from their heads, or the sunglint
and cloud in the car window, or that voice
as it murmured on, uninterrupted,
through the click and cough of the doors.

A Blackbird in Mining Country

We line up behind badly pocked shields
in a lull.
          But a blackbird
panics up from behind the six-deep line
we face and hurls itself across
no-man's-land towards us, babbling
its cranky alarm:
                 automatically,
those nearest go down to a crouch
beneath upraised and slanted shields,
a whole swathe flattened in our rank
like a path in the long grass pressed out
by the morning's breeze as we wait
for buses bringing the hooded men.

The Three Rioters

(a version from Chaucer)

Then one of the rioters, the most proud,
snapped right back, "What d'you say? Stuff it!
Why do you keep your ugly mug muffled?
You're so old and raddled you ought to be dead".
But the old man turned back. He nodded his head.
"I've been to the limits of this great earth
and found no living soul – that's the truth –
in the teeming city, or any quiet place,
who'd change their light youth for this, my age.
So I'm forced to stumble round in this state,
bent, imprisoned, for whatever time's set.
I can't give myself up to death either.
Will you let me pass? I'm a restless creature
beating at my mother's gates, at this earth.
Incessantly I tap-tap with this white staff
and call out *Mother! Mother! Let me in!*
Look how wasted I am – flesh, blood, skin.
Let me know when I can rest this filthy bag
of rotten bones. Mother! Take away these rags
I've used to cover myself with far too long.
Give me a simple sheet to wind myself in.
But she won't do me even that good grace.
So my flesh is grey, my skin is creased.

But listen will you, don't you know it's rude
to insult someone so on the public road,
unless they've insulted you, or done you wrong?
Don't you know your Bible? There's a line,
'When the grey-haired elder visits your house
rise in respect'. Just you take my advice:
don't go doling out hurt to any old man
unless you want people to do you harm
when you're my age – if you get so far!
Well – now God be with you, whoever you are."

"Huh, you old git! Jesus! What a fool!"
cried one of the men. He thumped the wall.
"Don't leave so quickly, old man. Bloody hell!
What you said just then – that bugger death –
we've got it in for him. Don't make me laugh –
I know you, old man – reckon you're his mate.
Tell us where he is or we'll make you pay.
I'm fucking certain you're part of his plan
to kill off – you bastard – all us younger men."

"All right", said the old man, "if it's death
you're so eager for, take this crooked path
to that willow clump – I've seen him there.
He'll not hide. He'll make you welcome there."

The Gleaners

In the distance, a man
on a still horse gestures to where
the majority work, bending
like cattle to crop the ground.
Women scour the harvested field
for leavings, gathering bunches
of straw like bouquets, laying them
like wreathes into the sheaf, binding
the stooks for men to heave them
into a cart or on to the stacks
growing imperceptibly into the brown sky.

Nearer, in this stubble, two women
lean as one into the earth,
each pair of eyes knowing only the next
burnished filament, each
committed to the field, headscarves,
red and blue, caught
low in their bob-bobbing.

A third, winched almost upright,
pats her bouquet. The angle she makes
to the others, the one machine
of the gleaners, has her resolved
not to ask entry, nor acceptance,
but soon to insist they lift their heads,
scarved in the red and blue,
and imagine the artist.

At the National Gallery

What am I to do with these angels' wings,
with the literalness of these gaping heavens
and haloes in the early galleries?
No-one believes them. Beyond meaning,
they are absurd – mannered and posed figures
as unlikely as the nude's fig-leaf, the wooden
gestures of saints staring straight through you:
uncomfortable attitudes, seeming content
with their fantasies of transfiguration and myth.

Yet casual visitors walk right past. They're drawn
to quotidian scenes, the scruffy breeches, old hats
in later pictures where they scribble notes,
trying to capture the vanishing feelings
of viewing these captured moments
of vanishing things – the recognisable gesture
at an execution, on the river, in the boudoir.
And I with them, yet always end uncomfortably
tracing holiday strolls through Canaletto's
Venice or impatient somehow with men
who explain to their quiet partners about
dimension, distance and the need for accuracy.

But Van Gogh's crippled chair confounds them,
restores a sense of things perceived in ways
inconsistent with the camera, eyes jaundiced
only with being human and limited which is
other than the capture of fleeting things,
the stunned insect, and like verse that must
struggle to avoid its final stop: another fairy-tale
though there are no haloes, no heaven here.
And I go back to those old pictures to find
their appeal, uncovered, is the honesty, almost
innocence, time has forced upon them,

for what was then dogma is laughable now, or
almost so. Uncameralike, their contentment admits,
rather asserts in all self-consciousness,
other possibilities multiplying beyond the frame:

like the one candle, illuminating a room,
the gleaming tabletop, across which one detailed,
serious face confronts another, unnaturally
bound in by a darkness in which we make out
nothing, yet know someone moves inches beyond
vision, rising, strained forward and demanding:
Give me some light, I say, lights! Now! A taper!

At Kavanagh's Bar, of course

He was the best storyteller in the land.
The first stumbling that he ever knew
was at ninety-eight, a stone-cold sober afternoon.
You're close to death, father, she said.

He smiled. *Death's blind drunk – he'll not catch me.*
Years later, left single-handed once more,
she stays close to the Ballinskelligs,
in Kavanagh's Bar, at Cahirciveen.

She says there's a snap of herself and Behan
on a big Dublin street, their breath in clouds.
She offers steaming potatoes in their skins.
She tells how she's seen red campion reeling

beyond White Strand – or was that maybe the day
they bucked across the Atlantic to an island
weathered like a man flat out on his back,
hands propped on his chest as if he'd pray?

No chance to reply. Squeezed on the bench,
*There's some men I wouldn't mind their boots
in my bed.* A Yankee she once walked out with –
down a field snow-drift deep in mushroom –

she made him take off his trousers and tied
the legs and filled them, bulging, to the fly.
To cap the day – she winks now – he walked home
in's swanky shorts. There's no Troubles here,

though there's one last tale like a crock of gold.
How one night two men perched on these stools,
eye to eye, two wet foreheads pressed together,
and swopped songs from both sides, being drunk.

The Return to Héloïse

(Saint-Preux returns to the dying Julie:
La Nouvelle Héloïse*)*

Secrecy and discretion must be preserved,
I know. The polished, panelled door
whispers perfectly shut. The informed maid
leads me through spacious unlit rooms.
Chandelier-shapes seem unsupported, floating
below the ceiling's shadow. They usurp
all remaining light and gleam, remembering
a glory spread below only hours before.
Long ago I passed through these rooms,
this interior dusk, this same hour, secrecy,
this trembling of nerves, to what seemed
the seal upon my life, why this loom
of clay was strung, thoughts woven,
to a secretive conjugation of eager flesh.

Only now am I forgiven.
After years I unlatch your door: the bed's
drapes tremble in the drifting light
of one candle; the room is crossed by shadows
as it was then; the silence, as it was then –
but this damaged, swaddled angel, eyes
ruined till no glimmer of recognition remains.
Love, your febrile heat burns, breathless,
one arm twisting in the counterpane,
hands, arms, face, scarring inexorably
with these eruptions already yellowing...
I'll take the hand, take and suck as if
harmless as the snake's kiss, for what poisons
an angel is elixir to man; this once,
knowing another world will prove refuge

for what shined briefly, too brilliantly here –
then kiss – swallow – inhale –
all flesh and thought hungering to be away
– though first the waiting and delirium:

euphoric, I glide from heavy door to door;
cross dim rooms to where the streets' fogs
deaden the stamping of horses.

George and the Dragon

1. *Uccello*

A boyish George, arrayed in gleaming plate,
lunges forward with lance and white rocking-horse.
The dragon's head dips in sympathy, bleeds
over the ground, on tousled patches of grass.

But she presents the beast with her palm out-
stretched as if a harmless pet pulled at the chain.
Is she deceived? Or is that fog behind
brave George, the black cave's echo, evil unseen?

2. *Moreau*

Again the white charger and armoured George.
The scaly dragon spilling its crimson blood
squirms on the long red lance. This time it's
the knight's scene alone: there's no more to add.

Even so, she squats in rocks at the back,
tall-crowned, impassive, not seeming aware;
but knowing the lance pierces George's heart,
and certain that, cowed, he will return to her.

The Bridegroom Watches Ships at Night

Long minutes after each hull has glimmered
out of the west and gone,
a foaming, ripped-edge of water
crawls towards him in a white pulse of rumour
off the deserted strait.

Waves break against the harbour wall
and wipe years from the blank slate of sand.
He's being pushed up to bed before time
with only the oldfashioned jigsaw
of their sharp-tongued struggles below.
Years later, sees his mother so frightened
she dare not touch the telephone
where it quivers in its cradle,
racked with the unflagging urge to tell.

He falls back to himself, the newly-wed,
knows in his head he's the last to know.
(He left her sleeping in their hotel room.)

The town trades its relentless gossip
as the bridegroom watches ships at night,
imagines in the waves' white, proliferating hiss
a cork now plucked down, spat out.

To the Painter, 1603

(for Ken Smith)

Sword, clipped beard, ruff:
and it's a nice twist that you
should have control of my posterity,
how I'll be seen, perhaps understood.

I know your business, my painter.
I know how many times you visit
my wife's bed, her warm body.
But she is mine, and will always be –

as you must, until I decide
to sever our convenient connection.
It will be my children alone,
painter, who survive into inheritance.

Then it's a twist I can regard
calmly – catch that in the eyes! –
that I must owe this other posterity
to your deft and gentle hands.

Air-Waves

As I slowed up and shifted down gear,
a dance song thumping from the car radio
was stretched out and smashed to pieces.

But we barely noticed that first time –
all eager to see the house, where it stood
beneath the surfing crackle of the pylons.

The girls loved the sight of so much sky.
They slipped into new schools with ease
though Sue and I made it home more slowly.

And by then, there was Stephen, almost four,
suddenly ill, his rush of growing gone awry,
and the doctor's face, closed up and dark

as the Manchester streets we had left behind.
He could tell me nothing. Inexplicable,
the pattern of disease. *A year – maybe two.*

Driving back across the hills, roadside wires
loop down, are yanked back to the blunted head
of each telegraph pole – and further off,

the pylons, hitching up skeins of darkness,
striding up country to a house where this car
and their sheaf of hot wires converge,

where a young man's voice on the radio
will melt down in a surge of boiling static
as I slow up, shift gear, and stop.

Insomniac

1.
My bed should creak like mummy
and daddy's then it would comfort
me but now like a hurt mouse
I hear it disturbing me,
makes me sleepless. Turn over,
and back. Turn the tired pillow
to its new cool face. Cover mine.
Twisting again, sit up and there
I am a shadow in a black room
in the dresser mirror showing
that I am asleep except my eyes.
If I could be rid of my eyes
I'd sleep and float like dark
into the dark – far away from
silent cats calling babies,
boots scuffling the path,
from a man's voice crying out
for an ambulance. *My arms*
he cried and I knew they'd
gone so I went to mummy and
daddy then. They were angry.
Still the hurt mouse squeals.

2.
She came in. The door cracked the room open
like an egg, spilling the light's warm gold
across our bed. She came with small steps
only so far as if she knew...and *mummy*
was all she'd say. Seeing her in silhouette
against the electric light worried me.
I shifted and caught sight of wet cheeks,
round, prominent and golden in that light.

It was some childish thing: a man
behind her door, hearing noises there
like the old dreams I sometimes had.
I hauled myself out of bed (he groaned
hissing through his teeth and rolled over).
I knew she was frightened – clutching
my nightdress till I thought it'd tear:
men were calling to her from nowhere.

I showed the empty garden. And staring down
at the pale lawn, its border's black shapes,
the curtain brushing my face, I was
small again, fighting the unsteady sense
of finding a sister as we stood, neither
wanting to move. Then, at last –
her cheeks drier now, though beginning
to crumple again as she went – I sent her
back to her own room. We heard no more.

The front part of my nightdress was damp
from her teary fingers. I slid back into bed
and reached for his turned white shoulder.

White-Out

(For Giotto, approaching Halley's Comet)

A bleb of silvery-pure spring water
unwinds itself along a silent corridor

from the blue planet to its destination,
the shock-headed comet, the white smear

across our sky. It cannot be hurried.
It is barely possessed of temperature.

One metre taller than a man, it has shaken
off our gravity to travel seriously.

It is a raindrop flung over my head,
being a subtle machine in a lucid sphere.

You – acute observer of the far – return
the restraint of your gesture to earth

where I've dropped the trace of responsibility
a while, where the wintery weather has

congealed to cloud and rain. Perfection's
a moving target here where I mark the blips

of this road's white line, the quarries
drowned for all the fishermen to explore,

the fact that the nation is a lava flow
boiling south. We struggle in the current.

There are rainstorms flung overhead.
My body refuses to fit in rented rooms

where I bend clumsily to recover a book
from the fireplace, my thin hips nudging

a brittle lamp from the mantelpiece
towards an almighty crash. I turn to it

quickly but remember myself possessing
such weightless calm and grace as I remark

each chip and fragment spilled on tiles
and hearth-rug, the dust of the explosion

rising like a smear of unexpected steam.
That evening, the story of two boys lost

under fog on the fells. They were found
squatting together under a lee, posed

to publicise outdoor pursuits, eyes crisped
with the frost, their flesh a mineral grin.

The Plait

Every word is explosive, brief,
shot deliberately from your bottled hoard.
I think you'd chatter if you were drunk;
you drink halves of dry cider, carefully.
You finger your twisted rope of hair,
pulled so fiercely tight its weight
seems to tug you backwards
as you probe ahead with a walking-stick,
pulling one leg behind.
                              Every movement
is so precise – to propel, or carefully steady –
there's no room for the wasteful signals
of what you feel, the accidental language
of hands and lips and tell-tale eyes.
Yet these are my supports.
Without them I grow slowly convinced
you find me stupid, full of social remarks,
stories with laughing interpretations.
Your reserve infuriates me –
but I'm terrified to beat it down.
You've had enough such able-bodied, helpful
violence on endless hospital wards.

Once, while we wound spaghetti on our forks,
you laughed and spoke in response to the moment,
not the logic of some scripted, inner scene
I'd had no chance to prepare –
and I asked what grudge of bitterness you felt
for being so unfairly, so crookedly born.

You gave nothing away.
                              I let the moment go.
I ducked beneath a joke as I saw you pull
your ship's-rope plait back into place,
a fierce vertical dropped like a ragged weal
down the length of your out-of-true back.

The Palio at Siena

(for Paul Mountain)

Remember no drunkenness.
Tread crackled brittle plastic
of emptied mineral waters
afterwards.

We drank steadily then.
Five hours of violent sun
boiled off in a single climate
of fuming sweat.

In the squeeze of memory –
such things are struck loose.
How people spilled barriers,
sprinted on the sandy track

after we had passed through
dense and heated air,
the sky glazed and senseless,
a matchless lens

zeroed on an immobilised crowd.
Couples in the gathering crush
are so turned on
by this mix of bodies

at cooking heat.
We share this equally:
saliva thread from lip to lip.
Mouths to naked glossy backs.

A woman pressed and wedged
so deeply in she drops
like an abandoned rag.
She keels precisely here

down through the airless
forest of planted feet.
Cannonblasts mark the time
with floated rings of smoke.

Where they dawdle overhead
the air seems cooler,
platonic and admirable.
Then why did you stay?

Whistles and arms leaven the air.
From the crushed ferment,
the particular reek
of one man's body,

eyes bird-like and sunk,
ignorant of the pelvis
arched to an isolated woman's back.
Tries to peel herself away.

He only goes elsewhere
while the jockeys struggle
for a starting-line and off
– a thumping

and fluttering
release –
we spin with the horses
drumming by, whips at work,

and over as quickly.
One weeping rider reins in,
absurd and gaudy pyjamas
flapping hard, and here,

people who have scaled
the barriers and hit out,
begin to wound each other,
stamp on legs and heads.

We cannot see the flags
waved in celebration,
nor the beaten, smashed,
the torn, sudden blood-spill,

scuffed dust on moistened skin,
nor the sudden, mysterious
business of feeling
for the old fool, reason

...with a free hand,
the cigarette I cried for
in this some kind of struggle,
plastered with others' wet

and hot breath
as if with fingers and hands,
(back broken, legs ache,
bent all but unwalkable now).

Say what kind of struggle.
Mark down here what kind...
Then why did you stay?
We grunt and grunt and shine.

Looking for an Old Man

(after Li Po)

Where red dogs bark
on the sodium ring-road
and traffic noise
blackens adjacent houses,
I've come to seek you.

In each garden I pass,
pale heads of bindweed.
The night is undistinguished.
The savour of coalsmoke
flattens across the kerb.

No-one here knows
which way you have gone:
two, now three lampposts
I've leant against.

Three Poems

(after Matsuo Bashō)

1.
In early evening
a large black bird
thumps to a precarious perch
on a rattling aerial.

Come midnight
under the city's purple sky
a wary cat shakes itself
from a ripped refuse sack.

I sat at this table
one frosty morning.
I chewed at the leftovers,
a pale dry *pitta*.

Tonight, wind struggling
at the hedge and gate,
I hear a leaking rain
overspill the gutters.

Cars hiss on the hill.
My insides are adrift
where I gaze into the bright
demanding rectangle.

2.
Tired of business.
Tired of the whole world.
I sit with a headless bitter
and a microwave pie.

Could any man lounge here
with autumn collapsing outside
and ignore the needle-prickle
of grey at his temples?

Nose down in water
sickeningly acid to taste,
a stray dog vainly relieves
its stiffening throat.

3.
From the flat below
a man's voice at five o'clock
each evening: a thud of music
and the lights come on.

Four cats – two above,
two below – fight for shelter
in this first wet spell
of the approaching winter.

Under the yellow pool
of our standard lamp, we eat
fish, bread, some late tomatoes.
We laugh it all away.

If there's nothing else
I've a roof over my head,
a thumb-nail garden,
a fruitless, clockwise plum.

The soporific note
of the last-invading wasps
betrayed no consciousness
of their quick-coming death.

Sleepy schoolchildren will
soon be trailing each other
under sodium streetlights
into assembly

and like an abandoned car
stripped of everything possible
I'll sleep on alone
(one night of the journey)

past time for breakfast
when TV personalities
sit in complete silence –
confronted by lilies.

As I stop-go-stop my way
to work, the radio urges
me more lonely still
with its three-minute worlds.

Behind me, in silence,
the white-washed walls
and some sheets of fresh paper
illuminate each other.

Rosetta

*'The Rosetta Stone provided the key to the
decipherment of ancient Egyptian writing.'*

*'Narrow
The heart that loves, the brain that contemplates,
The life that wears, the spirit that creates,
One object, and one form, and builds thereby
A sepulchre for its eternity.'*

Epipsychidion

1.
You come to me rich in deception.
You bring a wick of twisted flax,
a quail chick and a horned viper.

You carry a basket with a handle,
a loaf, two flowering reeds, water,
a mouth and a tethering rope.

It is promise of a safe anchorage
one day that you tempt me with
as the alphabet of gifts goes on:

here, folded cloth, there, a hawk,
the bolt from a door, a pool,
a jar-stand, a hill, a hand.

You say *I have shed so much light
there can be no shadow of a doubt
left now even in these lowest times.*

You encourage me with this gift
of an owl – old wisdom's bird –
because it sounds my name's initial.

But what else? You bring no map,
no code and no key, crowing,
no doubt, no dark, learn from me.

92

2.
When did the hieroglyphic die?
At what last click of which chisel,
what scratch of stylus or dousing

of which inky brush did old Egypt
begin her dumb millennium?
In the echoing of that small moment

imagine Pharaoh's voice mouthing
ever more obscurely *another remedy*
for preventing coming out a snake

its hole, another remedy preventing
and being buried under a dull
pyramid. Where is the quail chick?

Where the folded cloth? Where the owl,
the wick of twisted flax, where the hill?
Gone under, sealed up, quite still.

3.
High in the air, you travel
smoothly at a terrifying speed,
wrapped in metalwork, cables, fuel.

You must rattle down the road
with others, luggage already a weight
you must fight our gravity for.

Down, down. What is remaining
of your atmosphere is lost as you
adjust to ours, thick with drizzle.

I'll leave at half-past eleven,
which means I'll be touching down
at half-past eleven. Though only

a trick of our countries' times,
to me this is the act of a goddess,
stooping down out of your heady sky

to the earth's and my own difficulty.

4.
History records the details
of discovery: it was just lying
on open ground like a found poem.

Now a dull plaque commemorates
the place. Are we so hide-bound
by language that to substitute

one scrawled stone for another
is the height of our ingenuity?
Don't ask for the Rosetta road –

now they call the place Rashid.
In another version, Bouchard orders
a company of sullen, sweat-reeking

men from Napoleon's army
to break up old walls for a site
to build on the Nile's left bank.

C'est quoi ça? Ta gueule toi!
C'est le cul de Bouchard! Non!
Par là! Le roc inscrit en grecque.

The *Courier d'Egypte* reported
a significant find of inscriptions
in the sacred, the demotic, and Greek.

5.
You took off everything except
your wristwatch and came to me
saying you never slept without it.

Now the bed's late-morning smell
ferments with our warmth, is stirred
by your rising to the bathroom.

I watch the grey rain's tapping
at the window – the way it
stretches and bullies the daylight,

unbuilding older resolutions.
Yet it multiplies the perfections
we have made. It drives me

deeper to bed, cradling myself
for you only, your steps across
the landing. I open the bed to you.

I want love's sharp solution again.

6.
See, we exhibit the stone balanced
on a circular metal framework
so it appears free to revolve

this way or that at the crucial
moment like a gigantic magnet.
What it will indicate I don't know,

but I'll figure it soon enough.
Most days I sit here beside it
advising the public's hands off,

then move on when the buzz sounds.
See there, how people puzzle with it,
leaning across the iron rails

as if squinting down a dark well.
It's a job you daydream on –
and welcome someone who'll listen.

But after all this time, there is
something about its dull black lump.
You imagine him poring over it

in the shade, chip-chippering,
filling it up with all this
significance; next you imagine

the rainy London afternoon,
come in bleary after three jars,
and drowsing through till four,

then crackle, grind, a shadow's moved.

7.
So what? I'm Bouchard. I survived
the Emperor's army in 'ninety-nine
in stinking Egypt. I'd remember

the stone for another drink...
Was a black-haired woman who bit
her lip I fucked through July.

I'd lie in her bed like a pit.
Made her turn me over, her horny
fingers scribble across my back,

then down, down, find their home
stretching arse. And afterwards
I'd hammer quickly through her

so there'd be no time for talking.
I lapped up her crying out.
We'd been together almost four weeks –

longer and I would have stayed –
when two of my bloody idiot boys
turned up a stone thick with writing.

8.
I woke to find my whole day's
mood set long before I rose
to consciousness. Half-remembered

vicious dreams had trailed
their stink right through my head.
I nursed myself to the landing,

saw the shrill red scribbling
you'd fisted to your door last night:
WAKE ME   PLEASE   WAKE ME EARLY!

But as I knocked open the door
into the fragrance of your room,
you spun in the sheets, bare arm

up to your ratted hair, while he
lay quite still, hand at his throat,
blue eyes drilling the ceiling.

9.
Basalt slab as tall as a man,
black as night in praise of Ptolemy,
it stood prominently in the temple.

At its rounded head, the winged disc
of Horus, the two crowned cobras
of the Upper and Lower Egypt.

Below, Ptolemy himself consorting
with gods and goddesses,
the greatest of whom has drawn

his hawk-face close to the king's,
presents a long spear...
It measures 114cm in height.

It is now only 72cm wide
and 28cm thick. Missing
are the upper left corner,

the lower right corner and one
narrow section of right upper edge.
Only 14 lines of hieroglyphic remain,

corresponding to 28 of damaged Greek.

10.
Our language is an aftertaste.
It cannot be caught at the rise,
or on the flood – but snatched at

and lost on a different side.
Like two lines of remembered song.
Like the shards of a smashed pot,

retrieved from its numbered sites
and reconstructed. A creation
into the empty belly of which we can

peer at leisure. This is where...

11.
I expect to be with you
in the end. There will be no
thunder and lightning revelations,

for the more I learn the more surely
I see our secrets are kept more
securely. Then I make a promise

that some moonless night I'll creep
to where you lie, when no-one will
guess who might dare such a thing,

and steal you away, Rosetta,
press you to me, my obituary
and my last verse. I will set you

over an empty grave – *Here lies
forever entombed in the chilly soil* –
in some Highgate wilderness

where you can make firm your self-
possession that is already the silence
of a woman who suffers a man

above her in bed till he sleeps,
then gently eases herself to come,
subsiding to remote contented sleep.